MW01029325

COME TO THE MANGER
A Study Book

Copyright © 2008 by Abingdon Press.

Cover art: © 2008 Raymond Poulet / Artists Rights Society (ARS), New York / /ADAGP, Paris

Abingdon Press

ISBN-13: 978-0-687-64711-8

Manufactured in the United States of America

08 09 10 11 12 13 14 15 16 17—10 9 8 7 6 5 4 3 2 1

Introduction

Get a group of parents together, and it is inevitable that someone will begin to tell a story about the birth of one of their kids—especially if there are brand new parents in the bunch. I remember being in the delivery room when our first child, Hannah, was born and beginning the process of coaching my wife on how to breathe, just as we were taught in the childbirth class. I had taken copious notes and had reviewed them before going to the hospital. As labor intensified, I held her hand and, with no small amount of excitement, began to encourage her to breathe in and out slowly, when she turned to me and said, "Sweetie, please shut up." Turns out she knew how to breathe all on her own (she had been doing it since her own birth, it seems). When Rob was born a few years later, I put my feet up and watched a football game until it was time to play receiver.

Sometimes the stories parents tell are full of laughter and joy at a healthy birth, and sometimes the stories parents tell are tinged with fear and pain as they recall their anguish over a newborn struggling for life. What both kinds of stories reveal, though, is a deep love for the little ones who come into our lives and change them forever.

There is no greater birth story in the world than the one we celebrate at Christmas. It carries with it all the elements of a great story: anticipation, conflict, hope, heroes and villains, and a surprise ending. We can feel the joy and the pain with every verse, from the prophets to the Gospels. The birth, life, death, and resurrection of Jesus is a story that touches the deepest parts of the human soul, which is why, year after year, we tell it again.

Advent is a great time for us to gather and listen to those stories again, but we do so with fresh ears and with eyes wide open for new possibilities. The biblical stories are best understood when they connect with our own. As you read through this Advent study, you will encounter a few of my stories that bubble to the surface when I read these ancient texts. You will remember your stories, too; and I encourage you to share them with a group, with a loved one, or even in a journal.

So, let us all come to the manger and hear great stories about a marvelous birth. Oh, and if you want to hold your breath in anticipation, that's OK, too.

Seeing God's Face

Scriptures for Advent:
The First Sunday
Isaiah 64:1-9
1 Corinthians 1:3-9
Mark 13:24-37

We have had quite a baby boom at our church recently, with several families having newborns within the span of a couple of months. Besides filling up the nursery on Sunday mornings, one of the other benefits for the church and for me as a pastor is that I have the great privilege of bringing these little ones into the church community through the sacrament of baptism. That is always a special occasion—moms and dads beaming, grandparents snapping pictures, the congregation joyously responding with their commitment to support the child and her family as she grows to know God's grace for herself.

What is most fascinating to me, though, is that moment when I take the child from her mother's arms and hold her. No matter how agreeable the child is, there is a momentary panic in her eyes when she cannot see mom's face. Sometimes there is a whimper, sometimes a full-out wail; but most often the child quickly moves her focus to the face of the one who is now holding her. They seem to reach out instinctively to touch that new face in front of them. In my case, that face has a goatee ripe for grabbing and a microphone just begging to be pulled off.

Recent studies have shown that babies may be better at face recognition than adults. In fact, humans start out with the ability to recognize and remember a wide range of faces even among races or species different from our own.[1] Somehow, though, as we grow, we begin to lose our ability to recognize faces. My theory is that it is because we can become too self-focused and busy to pay attention to those around us.

The Scriptures for this first Sunday in Advent are all about recapturing the ability to recognize faces, particularly the face of God revealed in Jesus Christ. When we come to the manger, we are doing nothing less than seeking the face of God—a face that the Scriptures say will one day be revealed in glory to the whole world.

REVEALING THE HIDDEN GOD
ISAIAH 64:1-9

One of my all-time favorite movies is *Monty Python and the Holy Grail*. The story of King Arthur and his Knights of the Round Table gets a silly retelling in this goofy and sometimes irreverent spoof. I laugh out loud every time I watch it. In the midst of the movie's silliness, though, there is a scene that is unintentionally poignant.

As Arthur gathers his knights, he suddenly hears an angelic heavenly sound and looks up to see cartoon clouds parting to reveal a robed and bearded God wearing a crown and speaking in a thundering voice. If you were to ask a child (or even many adults) to draw a picture of what God might look like, the results would probably look a lot like the movie's version of God. After God tells Arthur to "stop groveling," God tells the king quite plainly that he is to set out on a quest to seek out the grail, the lost cup of Jesus from the Last Supper. Arthur replies that that sounds like a good idea, to which God thunders, " '*Course* it's a good idea!"

What strikes me about this scene is that the Python's parody of God is what a lot of people hope might be the reality. Wouldn't it be great, for example, if God would part the clouds and speak to us plainly, telling us what to do and what path we are to take with our lives? Some people I meet present this as a theological conundrum: If God is all-powerful, all-knowing, and omnipresent, why doesn't God just reveal himself to us and eliminate any doubt? Why all the secrecy?

The same question is asked by the writer of Isaiah, who entreats God to "tear open the heavens and come down" in an awesome display of power and might evident to all the nations (Isaiah 64:1-2). The writer saw God as living in the "holy and glorious habitation" of heaven but lamented that God seemed so distant, withholding God's "heart" and "compassion" from the writer and his people (63:15).

God had previously been present with his people in power, delivering them out of Egypt, leading them by a pillar of cloud and a pillar of fire, revealing God's glory in giving the Law to Moses on Mount Sinai, dwelling with Israel in the wilderness Tabernacle, inhabiting the Temple built by Solomon, going before Israel in battle, and doing more "awesome deeds" (64:3) that God's people had not expected. No one in history had ever heard of or seen a God so powerfully present and active on behalf of his people (verses 3-4). Now, though, as the people suffered from the sting of defeat and exile at the hand of the Babylonians, it seemed that God had closed up the clouds and turned off the fireworks on their behalf.

People want signs from God but tend to ignore them when they are present. Even while God was making the "mountains quake" at Sinai in Exodus 32, talking with Moses on the mountaintop, and giving him the Law, the people of Israel were at the bottom of the mountain complaining against God and Moses and crafting their own god in the form of a golden calf. No matter how spectacular the sign or evidence, humans are easily blinded to God's presence and power because of sin—the serious human drive for self-interest and self-indulgence. Sin has a way of blocking our view of God by putting up a mirror that causes us to fall in love with our own reflection.

Israel had continued that long history of neglecting God and going after other pagan gods; and for that, as the prophets had continually pointed out, there would be consequences. Exile was one of those consequences, but the greater problem was God's apparent retreat into hiding. The writer seems to have been conflicted about all this, even implying that God's hiding may have been the cause of Israel's sin in the first place (Isaiah 64:5). Did God hide from God's people because they had sinned, or had the people sinned because God had hidden from them?

The writer and his people felt the pain of God's absence. They had become unclean, and any "righteous deeds" they had done could not purify them. The *filthy cloth* here refers to a garment stained with menstrual blood, which was considered to be ritually unclean (Leviticus 15:19-24). Sin had caused the nation to dry up like a fallen leaf driven by the wind (Isaiah 64:6). No one prayed anymore or attempted to cling to God because God had "hidden [God's] face" from them and had given them over to the consequences of their sins (verse 7).

I once saw a quote—maybe it was on a bumper sticker—that went something like this: "If you feel distant from God, just ask yourself, 'Who moved?' " If God seems hidden to us, maybe it is because we have stopped looking for God in the midst of our daily lives. In the Scriptures, heaven is not a far away place "way beyond the blue" as the old song says; but rather it is God's realm, God's dwelling, and it is quite near to us. All we need to do is put down the mirror and open a window into the relationship God wants to share with us. Rather than a booming shout from the clouds, God more often is revealed in the "still small voice" (1 Kings 19:12, King James Version). We can hear if we are focused enough to listen.

Advent reminds us, too, that if we want to see the face of the hidden God, we do not do so by looking up for a heavenly sound and light spectacular. Rather, we find it by looking into the dark recesses of a stable and into the eyes of a humble, helpless child.

"We are the clay," said the writer of Isaiah, and God is the potter (64:8). We must not give into the temptation of sin to make gods in our own image. Instead, we submit ourselves to the potter, who can mold us into his own spitting image.

When have you felt distant from God? What are some of the awesome deeds God has done in your life that you may not have recognized before as such? What sin do you need to confess in order to draw closer to God?

REVEALING THE LORD
1 CORINTHIANS 1:3-9

One of the most vivid memories of my childhood was the Saturday after Thanksgiving when my mother and grandmother would bundle my sisters and me into our snowsuits and drive into Pittsburgh for the annual holiday shopping trip. Even before the turkey hit the freezer on Thanksgiving Thursday, I started dreading this trip. The problem as I saw it through my ten-year-old eyes was that my mom's idea of Christmas shopping and mine were radically different. To me, spending a couple of hours in a toy store trying out all the new stuff would be time well-spent. After all, then I would know what I wanted Santa to put under the tree.

Mom's idea of shopping, though, was dragging us through as many large department stores as possible, having us try on all manner of clothing—usually consisting of polyester dress pants and shirts with lots of buttons. I would be so bored that Saturday that I would not notice Mom stuffing all those bags in the trunk of the car and that those same pants and shirts were the ones I opened quickly on Christmas morning before moving on to the good stuff—kind of like eating your vegetables before dessert.

Still, Mom always promised us that if we were good and kept moving our little feet from store to store, we would get to sit on Santa's lap at the end of the day and tell him that we did not want any more socks, thank you very much. That motorized fire truck I saw in the store window would do quite nicely. With visions of the jolly old elf dancing through my head, I trudged along the streets of the Steel City through the soot-covered snow with about as much determination as a boy can muster.

Looking back, I do not remember any of the toys that I asked for; but I do remember being fascinated by the city. The window displays were beautiful. The streetlights glowed in the fading afternoon light. People waited in large crowds to cross the street. Each department store piped Christmas music to speakers out on the street; and everywhere you could hear the sound of bells ringing, because on nearly every busy street corner and in front of Horne's,

Gimbel's, Kauffman's, and all the other stores, a bundled person rang a big silver bell next to a red Salvation Army donation kettle. My mom could never pass one without dropping something in. We were a working-class family, but Mom knew that there were plenty of others out there who were less fortunate than we were and that we needed to help them. I remember thinking that it would be great to give them all those extra dress socks.

Christmas shopping nowadays is quite a different experience. It is easier to shop by pointing and clicking your computer mouse than it is to drive downtown. Even if you venture downtown, most of the old stores have moved out. Stores in malls start putting up their Christmas decorations before the Halloween displays are down, which dilutes the whole season.

I read somewhere recently that the Salvation Army has been hit hard by the decline in kettles and even more so by the lack of ringers. In Knoxville, Tennessee, for example, the Salvation Army had to pay out about $30,000 to hire people to man the few kettles that would be around town during the 2006 Christmas season.[2] People need to hear those bells. The decrease in funding that this important charitable organization receives is alarming, but I think the greater problem is that in our culture the gap between rich and poor gets wider every day. People need to remember that while they are spending buckets of cash on Christmas, there are people down the street who do not know where their next meal is coming from. Those silver bells Bing Crosby used to sing about were not only a sure sign of "Christmas time in the city," they were also a ringing reminder to everyone that the season is supposed to be about giving more than receiving.

When I read Paul's greeting in his letter to the Corinthian church, what leaps out at me is his repeated references to "the Lord Jesus Christ." The name of Jesus is referenced eight times in the first nine verses of 1 Corinthians 1. To me, the name sounds like the repeated ringing of a bell reminding the Corinthian church to whom they belonged and to what mission they had been called.

At the time of Paul, Corinth was one of the most cosmopolitan cities in the Roman Empire. A Roman colony about 40 miles from Athens, Corinth sat on the narrow isthmus of the Peloponnese, which put the city in a strategic economic position. Ships wanting to avoid the stormy middle of the Mediterranean Sea would tack closer to the coast and dock on one side of the isthmus. From there, the ships were portaged a couple of miles overland, cargo and all, and launched safely on the other side.

The constant flow of sailors and travelers in and out of the city made some of the citizens wealthy. However, unlike the circumstances in other cities in the empire, this wealth was known for being devoid of culture. Unlike Athens, Corinth was not so much a center for learning and the arts as it was a place where one could engage in more worldly and pleasurable pursuits. With all the sailors coming through town, along with other people seeking their fortunes, and with the proliferation of a variety of pagan religions and fertility cults that practiced temple prostitution, Corinth developed a reputation as a morally lax city. The burgeoning wealth of the most prosperous citizens also resulted in the mistreatment of the poor, giving Corinth the distinction in the rest of the Roman world as a city that lacked compassion and grace.

Paul had arrived in Corinth sometime around the year A.D. 50 and established a church. The makeup of that church was mostly Gentile, which we can deduce by the number of Greek and Latin names Paul mentioned. Like the rest of Corinth, however, the church reflected the steep divide between the rich and the poor. The social divide was causing problems in the young church with the rich, who did not have to keep working hours, often arriving early at church dinners and eating all the choice food before the working-class members could get there (1 Corinthians 11:17-34). Also causing division in the church was the issue of spiritual gifts as some of the believers believed themselves to be superior in their giftedness (12:1–14:40). Paul clearly had his work cut out for him as he tried to bring together this divided church.

Using the standard conventions of ancient letter-writing, he began with thanksgiving for the believers. Paul's thankful words, however, are a kind of thesis statement for what he would address later in the letter. Paul reminded the Corinthians that God's grace had been given to them in Jesus Christ (1:4), that they had all been "enriched" in "speech and knowledge" (verse 5), and that they had all been "strengthened" and given spiritual gifts (verses 6-7). From the outset, Paul wanted them to realize that the cultural and economic divides that separated the classes in the city were not to be part of the church's life and fellowship.

Like a ringer on a busy street corner, Paul used the repeated name of Jesus as a clarion call and a reminder that everyone is equal in Christ, that everyone falls under the lordship of the true King of the world. *Lord* was a title usually reserved for Caesar, but Paul liberally applied it to Jesus, who will wield ultimate authority over the whole world. When the true Lord is revealed in the end, on the "day of our Lord Jesus Christ" (verse 8), everyone will be judged, not by their wealth and power but by their faithfulness to God and their care for others. The Christian life is not about status or about having more; it is all about Jesus.

Understanding that we are all under the lordship of Jesus Christ is probably the most important message we can remember during this season. We need to think about how much our spending, our attitudes, and our desires reflect the culture around us instead of reflecting the call of Christ. If the name of Jesus is not ringing in our ears as we approach the Advent season, perhaps we need to stop shopping and start listening for the bells. How we live our lives, how we approach those who are poor, and how we spend our money and our time are all reflections of who is the Lord of our lives. May the name of Jesus be in our ears, on our lips, and in our hearts as we await his coming.

Where can you contribute your time, money, and effort to serving the poor in this season and beyond? How can you keep the name of Jesus before you in the midst of all the holiday chaos? How does your spending reflect your discipleship?

REVEALING THE
TRUE MESSIAH
MARK 13:24-37

Prior to experiencing my call to ministry, I served for about ten years as an enlisted man and an officer in the Army National Guard. While it was not a full-time job, I did spend a lot of time in the field as a "light infantry" soldier, which, in military-speak, means that you walk everywhere instead of riding. The irony is that a "light" soldier is expected to carry up to 75 pounds worth of gear into battle. With that much on your back, one does not walk so much as lurch through the bush.

As an enlisted man, one of the jobs I found to be the most difficult was sitting on the observation post, or "OP," at night. When the platoon is drawn into a defensive perimeter, the soldiers on the OP are placed outside the perimeter to act as a kind of tripwire, alerting the rest of the platoon to any enemy troops sneaking up on them in the darkness. While soldiers within the perimeter are usually at 50 percent security (half of them asleep, half awake), the OP must stay alert and vigilant 100 percent of the time. Pulling OP duty means you are going to be in for a long night.

Out there in the dark you are alone except for a buddy, with whom you cannot talk lest you give away your position. You spend hours staring into the darkness, waiting for something to happen while simultaneously praying that nothing does. Sounds become magnified; and fixed objects, such as trees, can appear to move if you stare at them long enough. After a full day of busting brush and digging in, you are locked in a battle to stay awake; and you find yourself daydreaming about sleeping. The orders are clear, however. You are to stay alert, stay engaged, and be ready for anything. The rest of the unit is depending on you to warn them of impending disaster.

I remember those long nights whenever I read this passage from Mark's Gospel. Jesus sounds like a company commander here issuing orders to his disciples to prepare them for a disaster that would occur within their lifetimes.

While it is easy to read Mark's "little apocalypse" in Chapter 13 and see it as a prediction of the end of the world, the context is more immediate than that. Jesus' warnings here are focused on the coming destruction of the Temple and most of Jerusalem by the Romans, which would occur in A.D. 70 after the revolt by Jewish rebels. Ever since the Romans had conquered Palestine under Pompey in 64 B.C, an undercurrent of revolution and messianic expectation had been bubbling in certain quarters of first-century Judea. Before and after Jesus, there emerged various revolutionary leaders who were seen by their followers as the new messiah who would kick out the imperial invaders. As quickly as each movement flared, however, the Romans would hunt down the leader, crucify him, and scatter the rest.

These revolutionaries are referred to in Greek as *leistes* in the Gospels—a term that is often translated as "thieves" or "bandits"; but it means much more than that. *Leistes* also referred to those who sought to bring God's reign and rule back to Israel by overthrowing the Romans through insurgency and military force. Jesus had viewed the Temple itself as the iconic symbol of these revolutionary ideas. "My house shall be called a house of prayer for all the nations," said Jesus as he turned over the tables of the moneychangers, "but you have made it a den of robbers [*leistes*]" (Mark 11:17).

Jesus no doubt had observed some of these revolutionary movements, many of which originated in his home region of Galilee. Jesus would in fact use revolutionary terminology in his own preaching. The phrase *kingdom of God*, or *kingdom of heaven*, was a kind of revolutionary slogan, which meant that God's reign and rule was coming on the earth and to Israel in particular. Jesus used the term freely, which resulted in the crowds following him and believing he might be the Messiah. Jesus, however, was working out a completely different messianic program than they had expected. Jesus himself would be charged with sedition against Rome and was crucified between two *leistes*, yet he would predict that this would not be the end of his messianic claim. The Temple would be destroyed, but a new one would rise in its place in the person of the risen Christ himself. The cross and the Resurrection would, in fact, vindicate Jesus as the real Messiah who brings forth God's revolutionary reign not with the force of arms but with a change of the heart.

Jesus saw the events lining up that would lead to the destruction of the Temple and gave his disciples their warning orders. Interestingly, like in a military operation, those orders are given in code. Apocalyptic language functions as a kind of symbolic shorthand in the Bible, using graphic symbols to point to larger events. In Mark 13:24-26, Jesus borrows apocalyptic images from the prophets Isaiah (Isaiah 13:10; 34:4), Ezekiel (Ezekiel 32:7-8), and Joel (2:10, 31), who used symbolic signs in the heavens to illustrate the cataclysmic events that were taking place in their own times as empires rose and fell.

One of the keys to understanding Jesus' focus in this passage has to do with his use of the title *Son of Man*, which Jesus borrowed from the apocalyptic Book of Daniel and applied to himself. The phrase "the Son of Man coming in clouds with great power and glory" is a direct reference from Daniel 7:13. In Daniel's apocalyptic vision, *Son of Man* means, literally, "one like a human being" who acts as a divinely appointed representative of God. In that particular passage, though, the Son of Man's "coming in the clouds of heaven" is not described as a return to the earth but about his coming to God after doing battle with the forces of evil. The Son of Man is thus exalted through faithful suffering on behalf of God and God's people. From the perspective of Jesus, his message and mission—characterized by faithful suffering and victory over the forces of sin and death—

would be vindicated. The cross would be his coronation and the Resurrection the coming of the true Messiah to God and the revelation of his victory to the whole world. The story of Jesus' triumph would be taken by his angels (also translated "messengers") to the "ends of the earth," gathering in those who would believe and follow the true Messiah in his revolutionary program of love. The Gospel of John puts it even more plainly when Jesus says, "And I, when I am lifted up from the earth, will draw all people to myself" (John 12:32).

Using the apocalyptic code of imagery and language, Jesus was telling his disciples to be ready for their whole world to change. Indeed, their generation would not "pass away until all these things have taken place" (Mark 13:30). It was not going to be the ultimate end of the world, but the destruction of the Temple would certainly be the end of the world as they knew it. They were to be ready, to be as watchful as a "doorkeeper," as alert as a soldier peering into the darkness, for the day when God would turn apparent danger and destruction into triumph.

While this passage may not be about the end of the world, the orders Jesus gave are no less valid to us. The destruction of the Temple was merely a foretaste of God's coming judgment on the whole world. It is easy to look at our world and see that in so many ways we are headed for disaster, but as Christians we also realize that things will not always be this way. We await the day when God's kingdom will be fully realized, when the face of Jesus will be revealed once and for all—the day when human systems of corruption and domination will no longer have control, the day when the first will be last and the last first, the day when God sets the world to rights, the day when the resurrection of the Son of Man is made real in the resurrection of us all.

In the meantime, we are called to be ready, to be prepared. Do not mistake that readiness for passive waiting, however. The task of the people of God is to work for what we pray for in the Lord's Prayer—making God's kingdom as real "on earth as it is in heaven." Do that, and when Jesus returns we can all join the band R.E.M. in singing, "It's the end of the world as we know it, and I feel fine!"[3]

I like that the Revised Common Lectionary puts this passage squarely in the first Sunday of Advent. In the midst of all the preparations for the coming of the Christ Child, we are reminded that this is one dangerous Baby—one who will upset the status quo, one who will suffer at the hands of people who saw him and his message as a threat, one in whose death and resurrection we somehow find new life for ourselves and salvation for the world.

In what ways is following Jesus a revolutionary idea in the present world? What are you doing to "keep awake" and be prepared for the coming kingdom of God?

---

[1] From "Baby Face: Infants Know Who You Are," at CNN.com, May 16, 2002 (www. archives.cnn.com/2002/HEALTH/parenting/05/16/baby.brains/index.html).
[2] From "Ringing in the Holidays With the Salvation Army," by Millete Birhanemaskel in the Knoxville News Sentinel, November 21, 2007 (www.knoxnews.com/news/2007/nov/21/ringing-holidays-salvation-army).
[3] From "It's the End of the World as We Know It (and I Feel Fine)," by Bill Berry, Peter Buck, Mike Mills, and Michael Stipe (R.E.M.) on the album Document (1987).

The Way to the Manger

Scriptures for Advent:
The Second Sunday
Isaiah 40:1-11
2 Peter 3:8-15a
Mark 1:1-8

Every year around this time people ask why we do not sing a lot of Christmas carols in worship during Advent. After all, everyone starts hearing those familiar songs of the season earlier and earlier each year; and stores start putting out their Christmas displays near Halloween. When people come to church they expect to sing about the newborn Babe in the manger, even as they are finishing Thanksgiving leftovers.

However, while the culture is ready to jump down the chimney or head to the manger while the leaves are still turning, the church calendar focuses on another aspect of the season. The four Sundays of Advent were brought into the tradition of the church as far back as the year 480 as a kind of second, though less austere, observance of Lent in preparation for the Christmas feast. Advent has historically been a time of waiting and preparation for the coming of the Christ, a time of penitence, prayer, and reflection. Celebrating Christmas without going through Advent is kind of like buying a book and reading the last chapter first—you know how it turns out, but you do not have any context in which to put the story. Advent provides the context for the Christmas story, helping us celebrate it more fully because we understand what it means.

When we read the Scriptures for the second Sunday in Advent, we do not hear the angels singing just yet. Instead, we hear the voices of the prophets who call God's people to prepare for the coming of the Christ. Instead of carols and bells, we hear the echoes of the biblical story of Israel. We hear about its need for a messiah, a savior who will liberate them from domination by foreign powers, but even more, a savior who will deliver all of humanity from enslavement to the effects of sin and death. Instead of singing the songs of Christmas, Advent calls us to listen to God's plan for redeeming the world.

As you read these Scriptures for the second Sunday in Advent, turn down the Christmas carols for a while and listen for that lone voice that cries out in the wilderness, "Prepare the way of the Lord." It is that voice that will show you the best way to the manger.

THE WAY HOME
ISAIAH 40:1-11

This passage from Isaiah 40 is familiar to many as one of the centerpieces of Handel's *Messiah*. I once served a church where the tradition was for all the church choirs in the community to come together in our church sanctuary on a Sunday afternoon during Advent and sing through the whole work. One of the coveted roles that day was that of the tenor who got to sing the solo "Comfort Ye, My People." Since I am not much of a singer (I think the whole "make a joyful *noise*" thing was directed at me), I always marveled at the effort it took to bring out the beauty of the piece.

Truth be told, though, I have never been much of a classical music aficionado. In the fifth grade, I picked up a pair of sticks and have been playing the drums ever since. I played in the high school marching band, in the jazz band, and with a variety of rock and country bands over the years. I am still playing with our church's

praise team. Drums in classical music generally require a lot more nuance and subtlety from the player than laying down a steady backbeat for a blues tune. I was once selected to play percussion for an honors orchestra in high school; but when the pieces we were given required our section to play about four measures out of a 30-minute symphony, I felt that my selection to the orchestra was a dubious honor. I confess that we percussionists played cards during rehearsals while counting out successive blocks of 120 measures of rest. So, while I hear the clear voice of a tenor in the back of my mind when reading Isaiah 40 I cannot help but hear a steady drum beat as well. In fact, when I read this passage closely, it feels more like a parade than a concert.

Some biblical scholars have come to see the whole book of Isaiah as being divided into two distinct parts, with Chapter 40 marking the beginning of "Second Isaiah." The first 39 chapters of the book concern the coming victory of the Babylonians over the kingdom of Judah, with the prophet telling the king Hezekiah that "the days are coming when all that is in your house, and that which your ancestors have stored up until this day, shall be carried to Babylon; nothing shall be left, says the LORD" (Isaiah 39:6). Isaiah's prophetic prediction would become reality as the Babylonians conquered Judah in 597 B.C. They exiled Judah's King Jehoiachin along with the royal family and other elites and replaced the king with their own puppet ruler, Mattaniah, whose name they changed to Zedekiah (2 Kings 24:14-17). The Babylonians destroyed the Temple and much of Jerusalem in 586 B.C. after a revolt led by Zedekiah and took the king and many who were left in the city into exile in Babylon (2 Kings 25:1-21; Jeremiah 52:4-27). The Temple was in ruins. Jerusalem and the surrounding areas were virtually empty except for the poorest people who were left behind "to be vinedressers and tillers of the soil" (2 Kings 25:12).

In the midst of this despair, though, the writer of Second Isaiah brought a word of hope to those in exile. Using the language of the law court, God proclaimed that the people of Jerusalem had served the term of their imprisonment, that they had "received from the LORD's hand double for all their sins" (Isaiah 40:2). The people and their kings had been unfaithful to God, had chased after idols, and had failed to treat the poor with justice. The Exile had been a reversal of their self-serving fortunes, but God's wrath had not been the final word. Instead of God's anger or a vitriolic form of "I told you so," God "speaks tenderly" a word of hope to God's people. The day was coming when the people would be allowed to return, to begin again, and to be restored in right relationship with God. I can almost hear God singing quietly in a clear tenor voice.

With verse 3, however, the percussion section takes over and the march homeward begins. During their time in exile in Babylon, the people of Jerusalem and Judah had no doubt witnessed the spectacle of the triumphant parades of the Babylonian kings. In the ancient world it was customary for kings returning victorious from battle to process into the capital city in grand fashion, displaying the captured booty and slaves from the defeated nations. The triumphant procession would take place on the wide main highway into the city, with every obstacle removed to allow the full glory of the king to be seen by all. With their term of exile completed, the king's highway would become the way for the people to begin the procession home—a procession that would take place when the Persians under King Cyrus conquered Babylon in 539 B.C. Cyrus would allow the exiles to return home and rebuild their Temple (Ezra 1:1-8; Isaiah 45:1).

The "wilderness" and "desert" references in verse 3 seem to be meant to invoke the idea of a second Exodus. As the people of Israel had been brought out of slavery in Egypt through the desert to the Promised Land in the time of Moses, so now would they be liberated from exile in Babylon, traveling the desert wilderness once again to their true homeland. God would be at the head of the parade, revealing the glory of God to all the nations (Isaiah 40:5).

The drumbeat continues in verse 6 as God reminds the people that humans and their kings are temporary and feeble. The Exile proved that the people were like grass—here today and gone tomorrow. Kings and empires rise like flowers, showing their glory for a brief time but then fading again to dust. What remains, however, is the steady beat of God's covenant promises, God's word that will "stand forever" and never fail to offer salvation and new life to God's people in every generation (verse 8).

The great procession approached Jerusalem. As was the custom in the ancient world, heralds were sent ahead of the returning king, announcing his arrival and preparing the people of the city for celebration. God had won the victory; had redeemed God's people from their exile; and, even more so, had redeemed them from their sins. God is a mighty ruler and a tender shepherd who fights for and cares for God's people (verses 9-11). The triumphant parade is complete, but the cadence of God's love goes on forever.

Advent is an opportunity for us to pick up the rhythm of restoration and redemption that God has laid down over the course of human history. There are times when we are out of step with God, when we exile ourselves to a far country in our sin, our pursuit of other gods, which come in many forms. We spend our temporary and finite lives on things that, in the end, are even more temporary—material possessions, work that is self-serving, pleasurable pursuits that only satisfy our longings for a brief time. Advent reminds us that there is another way, the way home, the way back to God. God seeks to release us from the things, the attitudes, and the temptations that enslave us. God seeks to lead us through the wilderness of change into a bright future where we live under the guidance, protection, and love of the Good Shepherd.

God's call is steady and unchanging. Will you pick up the beat and get in step?

When have you felt out of step with God? What are the things that separate you from feeling at home with God? How will you pick up God's rhythm of restoration and love in the coming year?

THE WAY OF WAITING
2 PETER 3:8-15a

As a young infantry officer in the waning years of the Cold War, one of the most fatalistic and funny blocks of training I was given every year was a three-hour course on what to do if a nuclear device detonated near my defensive position. It was fatalistic because I knew that if that happened I was going to be toast. It was funny because despite that given reality, the Army still had a field manual procedure for me to follow.

At the start of the course, each platoon leader was given a pocket-sized mathematical chart that was called a "whiz wheel" with a ruler marked on the side. I was supposed to keep that in my rucksack "just in case" I saw a mushroom cloud nearby. If that were to happen, I was to do the following:

- Hunker down deeper in my foxhole. (No problem.)
- After the initial blast rolls by overhead, stand up and observe the cloud. (Really?)
- Reach into my rucksack and take out the whiz wheel. (Yeah, that'll be my first thought.)
- Use the ruler on the side of the whiz wheel to measure the cloud. (Not enough inches on it for that, sir.)
- Spin the whiz wheel, matching your distance from the point of detonation to the cloud, the wind speed, and the direction [and several other calculations that I can't recall] to determine the speed and direction of the fallout. (I'm sure my mind will be clear enough to do this higher math.)
- If my radio still works and, if my headquarters still exists, report the results of my calculations and await further orders. (Like, "Run"?)

Usually after the last step, one of the new lieutenants would ask the inevitable question: "Sir, will any of this really matter?" The instructor, a captain from the NBC (nuclear, biological, chemical) branch, always said the same thing. "No," he would deadpan with grave honesty (those guys are like that), "It's all simply designed to just give you something to do until your world comes to an end." Nervous laughter immediately filled the room as the young officer got the picture.

It is hard to fathom events that have that kind of finality. We have talked a bit already in this study about how the Gospel writers envisioned the cataclysmic events surrounding the destruction of the Temple in Jerusalem in A.D. 70 and what that meant to the early church. That event was the end of their world as they knew it, but they looked forward to a new age that was breaking in. The new age would come to fullness at the reappearance of the risen Jesus who would complete the work of justice and peace for the whole world that he began on the cross. The early Christians believed that the "day of the Lord" was imminent, that Jesus would return at any moment. Some, like the writer of Second Peter, believed that event would be characterized by a sweeping fire that would vaporize the existing heavens and earth, purging them and blazing the way for the new heaven and earth to come. The effect would be the equivalent of a nuclear explosion, leveling the old world to make way for the new.

The thought that the world would be destroyed by fire is rare in the New Testament. Fire was usually referred to as a form of punishment for the unjust (Matthew 13:40-42, for example). The writer of Second Peter may have been influenced by the contemporary belief of the Stoics that the universe cycled through destruction by fire and reemerged as a newly created universe like a phoenix rising from the ashes. Regardless of the origin of his belief, the writer's primary focus was to instruct the church to prepare for that day, not by hunkering in a spiritual and cultural bunker but by doing all the good they could do in getting ready for the world to come.

The biggest problem our instructors had was getting us field officers to believe that a nuclear strike would actually happen to us. Sabers were rattled by politicians all the time during the Cold War, but the thought of seeing mushroom clouds from our foxholes seemed impossible. We trained hard and learned our whiz wheels, but we joked about them instead of listening with grim determination. That was pretty naïve of us; but when you train for something over and over again that does not happen, you tend to lose a sense of urgency about it.

The same thing apparently had been happening to the Christian community to whom Second Peter was written. Some of those surrounding the church were scoffing that the return of Jesus had not happened despite all their anticipation. "Where is the promise of his coming?" they joked. "All things continue as they were from the beginning of creation" (2 Peter 3:4).

We look at our world and realize that day-by-day things do kind of look the same as they ever were. We look for something better, hope for it; but we open the newspaper, log on to the Internet, or turn on the TV and are greeted each morning with another daily dose of mayhem. If God has promised finally to do something once and for all about the pain and corruption of the present world, what is the hold up? Why keep training for something that does not look like it is going to happen any time soon, if at all?

For the writer of Second Peter, the answer to the skeptical questioning of some of the church rank and file was all about timing—God's timing versus the human need for instant gratification. For God, who is not bound by the limits of time and space, 1,000 years and a day are equal lengths of time (verse 8). Humans, who are bound by the day-to-day march of chronological time, have a hard time being patient; but for the writer of Second Peter, the waiting is an opportunity.

The Lord has delayed in coming, not out of "slowness" but out of a desire that everyone should "come to repentance" (verse 9). God is presenting an opportunity for training, preparation, and a change of heart and mind for all people so that when the day of the Lord comes, it will not be the devastating conflagration that many anticipate. Instead, it will be the realization of a promised hope (verse 10). The explosive fire that is coming, says the writer, will burn off the impurities of humanity, exposing evil and destroying it once and for all, leaving behind newly refined heavens and earth "where righteousness is at home" (verse 13). In the meantime, we are to act as people who have already been refined and purified by "leading lives of holiness and godliness" (verse 11).

I once saw a bumper sticker that said, "Jesus is coming . . . look busy." Indeed, when Jesus comes, what will he find us doing? Will we be hunkered down in our Christian bunkers, fatalistically waiting for the end of the world; or will we be up and moving about in the world, training and working urgently to bring the life of the new heavens and the new earth to the present world? Advent is a call to put down the end-time whiz wheel and pick up God's vision for the renewal of God's good creation!

If Jesus were to return today, what would he find you doing? How might you help to bring new life to the present world?

THE WAY
OF REPENTANCE
MARK 1:1-8

One of my seminary classmates was appointed to serve a couple of rural country churches after gradua-tion. The larger of the two churches was situated near a mountain stream in the Appalachians, and every Pentecost Sunday it was that church's tradition to hold a bap-tismal service in one of the deer pools in the creek (pronounced "crick" in that part of Pennsylvania) for any who desired to be immersed. In late May or early June, the creek was still running a little high; and the water temperature reflected the winter snows seeping into the ground water at the source.

During one of these baptismal services, an older man waded out into the water to receive the sacra-ment. My friend ducked him under the still frigid water using the traditional liturgy; but before the pastor could finish the words "I baptize you in the name of the Father, Son, and Holy Spirit," the man shot out of the water, sputtering and gasping, "Man, that shocked the devil out of me!" My friend, not missing a beat, said matter-of-factly, "Well, that's the point."

The beginning of the Gospel of Mark could be said to have the same kind of effect. Unlike Matthew and Luke, there is no Christmas story with shepherds, angels, or magi. Unlike John, there is no poetic theological pre-amble. Mark simply begins with "the good news of Jesus Christ, the Son of God" and then immediately whisks the reader to the Jordan River and the shocking message of John the Baptist.

On the way to the Jordan, Mark borrows two quick verses from the

Hebrew Bible to describe the prophet's mission and message. The mission is laid out in Mark 1:2, which the writer attributes as a quote from Isaiah; but actually it is more like an alternate reading of Malachi 3:1. In that particular passage, the messenger was to be the one who would purify and restore the priesthood to its rightful place and function in the Temple. John, operating in the wilderness of Judea miles from the Temple, was performing a ritual of purification and restoration for the whole nation of Israel. John's message is summarized in Mark 1:3, which does quote from Isaiah 40:3. He was to be "the voice crying out in the wilderness" preparing "the way of the Lord." It is not clear at this point whether John knew how or in who the Lord would come, only that a major God-promised shift in the balance of power was soon coming. In the meantime, John warned the people that they needed to get ready by repenting and being cleansed of their sins.

That John preached and baptized out in the wilderness and not in Jerusalem or another more accessible and visible location puzzles modern readers. The Judean wilderness is a barren and desolate place and at that time was widely known to be home to wild animals, bandits, nomads, and the occasional religious hermit. If you lived in Jerusalem, going to the Jordan was not a simple day's journey, but one fraught with danger and discomfort. Leaving the relative safety of the hill country, one had to travel about 18 miles down to the Jordan River, going from about 2,700 feet in elevation in Jerusalem to more than 1,300 feet below sea level where the Jordan flowed into the Dead Sea. Still, the "people from the whole Judean countryside and all the people of Jerusalem" were traveling out into the desert wastes to hear John and to be baptized by him.

We read about John's clothing and diet and wonder why anyone would go to all that trouble to hear him preach. We like our presenters to be well-groomed and media savvy, but in first-century Judaism most people would likely have recognized John's lifestyle and location as a clear echo of the prophets of old.

In Jewish thought and history, salvation always came from the wilderness. Moses, Elijah, and David—three of the most important people in the Hebrew Bible— had to flee into the wilderness at times; but they emerged from the desert to lead their people. In the wilderness, God strengthened them for their mission. After his baptism, Jesus went into the wilderness to prepare for his ministry (Matthew 4:1-11; Mark 1:12-13; Luke 4:1-13). The past leaders of Israel had emerged from the desert, so when John began to preach there, the people took notice.

John's wardrobe also reflects the prophetic tradition. Elijah had been "a hairy man with a leather belt around his waist" (2 Kings 1:8) and spoke as God's forerunner. John's clothing of camel's hair and a leather belt would have been an unmistakable symbol to the crowds who came. As for his diet, I learned on a recent trip to the Holy Land that the carob tree was also known as a "locust" tree and the edible pods were referred to as "locusts." This may soften the image of a wild-haired prophet munching on bugs for lunch; but he was, nevertheless, a man of the wilderness.

While John the Baptist is a compelling figure in his own right, his baptism may have been the bigger draw. Ritual bathing was a common and repeatable practice throughout first-century Israel. *Mikvahs*, or bathing pools, have been excavated in many of the important Jewish sites of the period. In Qumran, for example, there are several such baths; and the Dead Sea Scrolls reveal that baptism was joined to the confession of sins. However, most ritual bathing was done by the individual without assistance. John seems to have taken that understanding of baptism and moved it from a mere individual act to one that was a sign for the whole nation of Israel— that repentance was needed for the whole nation because God's judgment was coming.

John's ministry of baptism in the Jordan River connects to the larger narrative of Israel itself. The most important story in the Hebrew Bible, next to Creation, was the Exodus. God had led the people out of slavery in Egypt, through the waters of the Red Sea, through the desert wilderness, and through the Jordan into the Promised Land. By baptizing in the Jordan, John seemed to be evoking that story all over again through an acted parable. John was calling the people to leave behind a spiritual Egypt, their old life of slavery to sin, and come through the purifying waters of forgiveness so they might be free to once again live out the covenant promises of God as God's chosen people. John was preaching that the time was short, that God's judgment was coming in the form of a person greater than himself, who would baptize them with God's own Spirit (Mark 1:7). It was time to get in the water and prepare for the coming kingdom of God.

As Israel's representative, Jesus would go through the waters of his cousin John's baptism as a clear signal that he was going to carry out Israel's mission to its completion—to be the one through whom the whole world would be saved. The good news that Mark proclaims at the beginning of his Gospel is that God's kingdom, in the person of Jesus, had broken in—a new day was dawning.

For us, baptism is not only a sign of repentance and forgiveness, but also a commissioning to join Jesus in bringing the Kingdom, God's new reality, into the world. Jesus' command to his disciples to baptize people in his name was not merely about adding converts to a new religion, it was also a sign of a world awaiting its full redemption (Matthew 28:19). As we journey on the way to the manger, may we remember that Jesus has called us, his disciples, to shock the world with his redeeming love.

How does being baptized affect how you live your daily life? How can you "shock the world" with a message of Jesus' redeeming love?

A Vision for Vocation

Scriptures for Advent:
The Third Sunday
Isaiah 61:1-4, 8-11
1 Thessalonians 5:16-24
John 1:6-8, 19-28

One of the more puzzling and abnormal aspects of the Christmas season, at least to me, is that people seem to be overscheduled. Just try to put together a meeting or work on a project in December, and people have a ready response: "I'm just swamped getting ready for Christmas," they say. "Let's do that after the holidays." I hear this from people who are church members as well as from people who are not. Apparently, Christmas is an equal opportunity exhauster.

Maybe people feel that way because we have not collectively done Advent well. Advent is supposed to be a time of waiting, reflection, and penitence. It is a time for us to sort through what is most important as we prepare for the coming of Christ. Rather than rushing around, Advent calls us to stop and consider who we are and what we are to be about.

The Scriptures for the third Sunday in Advent seem to be designed to help us putall our activity into perspective and move it in the right direction. We should be working as diligently on our vocation as disciples as on our Christmas cookies as we wait for Jesus. As you read these Scriptures, think about your own busyness during this season. How is it preparing you to come to the manger?

THE MESSIAH'S MISSION
ISAIAH 61:1-4, 8-11

It is pretty common for people coming out of college these days to bounce around through a few jobs before settling on a particular career path. Even though I graduated from college during the Reagan administration, my own employment history is no exception. In addition to serving part-time in the military in those days, I also held jobs such as tour guide, collections agent, radio ad writer, and—most memorably—as a security guard.

I say memorable because at the time I was working in security I thought it was a pretty pointless job. I had a government security clearance, so I was hired to do night security for a firm that designed and manufactured electronics for the military. The stuff they made was so secret that many of the employees had no idea what it was used for, especially those of us working on the blue-collar end of the employee roster.

The job essentially boiled down to this: Walk around all night with a flashlight, and check to make sure that secure filing cabinets and doors were closed and locked. These doors and cabinets were spread over a massive, multi-acre complex, so it took a couple of hours to make one round. I would get a break and then do it again. At each secure location there was a keypunch station, so I had to punch the key into a paper recorder I carried around so I could prove I had been there. Other than the recorder, the only other piece of equipment I was issued was one of those long metal flashlights—the kind that takes four D batteries. That was it.

The first week on the job I asked my supervisor what I was supposed to do if, say, I came across someone rifling through a secure filing cabinet snapping pictures with one of those little spy cameras like you see in the movies.

He said, "You yell, 'STOP!' " And if they don't stop? "Then," he said sarcastically, "you yell 'STOP!' again!"

Thanks for the tip.

I spent a lot of hours walking around in the dark wondering who would actually care if one of those file cabinets were left open. Occasionally the guards would find one unsecured by a careless employee, but no action was ever taken on the reports we filed. After a while, we realized that no one cared that much about those cabinets or, for that matter, about us.

A recent poll showed that 77 percent of Americans hate their jobs, and one of the primary reasons why is that many employees do not see how their job fits into the big picture of the company's mission and purpose. The measure of job fulfillment is not as much about the level of compensation as it is about having a sense that what you do matters to someone—to *anyone*. It is little wonder then that we encounter bored and lifeless workers behind sales counters, in factories, in office cubicles, and in a host of other work settings. Without a sense of being an important part of something larger than ourselves, human will and enthusiasm can atrophy; and work, no matter what it is, becomes merely a necessary evil.

Surely God did not create us to live this way. We were made to reflect God's image, to be human "beings" rather than human "doings." Whether you are a security guard or a securities trader, it is important to remember that ultimate fulfillment happens when we see our lives as being bound up in the larger purposes of God for the whole world.

We begin to see that purpose when we stop thinking about our *job* and instead focus on our *vocation*. The word *vocation* comes from the Middle English word *vocacioun*, which implies a kind of religious calling. It is a word that has little to do with function and more to do with a response to meaning and purpose. If the word *job* implies a functional, task-oriented, time-dependent means of employment, then *vocation* implies a broader worldview where one's life is important because of purpose and call. To put it another way, a job is something you *do* from 9 to 5, but a vocation is something you *are* 24/7.

A prime biblical example of vocation is found in Isaiah 61, particularly in verses 1-3. The prophet has received a call from God to specific tasks—bringing good news to the oppressed people of Israel, mending hearts broken by years of exile, proclaiming their release from captivity, comforting the mourners, and announcing God's favor and God's judgment—those tasks grow out of the relationship of the prophet to God. Unlike an employee with a detached relationship with a supervisor, the prophet saw himself as being personally called by God to his prophetic vocation. God's Spirit was upon him, anointing him with the ability and energy to do the work, not out of a sense of obligation but with a divinely appointed purpose. The prophet and his work would find their fulfillment in furthering God's larger vision of justice for all God's people (verse 8).

When Jesus first went public with his ministry, he chose this prophetic call from Isaiah 61 to define his own vocation as the Messiah (Luke 4:18-19). Jesus regarded Israel as still being in exile, not through slavery in a foreign land but through slavery to the effects of sin and death. He had been anointed by God's Spirit in his baptism by John the Baptist in the Jordan (Luke 3:21-22), had gone into the desert for 40 days of temptation and preparation, and was now prepared to live out his vocation.

Jesus' ministry was to be an announcement of "the year of the Lord's favor" (Isaiah 61:2;Luke 4:19)—a reference to the Torah's call for a jubilee year on the 50th year occurring at the end of seven sabbatical cycles of seven years each. In that year, all land was to be returned to its ancestral owners and all Israelite slaves were freed (Leviticus 25:8-17, 23-55; 27:16-25; Numbers 36:4). In the Hebrew Bible, jubilee was understood as a major leveling of the economic and social playing field. For Jesus, the kingdom of God would be that and more, bringing down the powerful, elevating the lowly, healing the sick, and announcing God's grace and forgiveness of sins. The tasks of his ministry were ordered around the larger purpose of proclaiming God's kingdom, God's justice and peace, coming on the earth.

Jesus would empower his disciples with that same vocation. A crew of working-class men with regular jobs, such as fisherman and tax collector, would see their lives and their work as being subject to the larger purpose of bringing the good news of God's grace through Christ to the whole world.

No matter what tasks we do to earn a paycheck, if we are following Jesus, we are to see those tasks and our jobs as being part of our discipleship and part of the larger purposes of God. If you work the counter at a store, for example, a positive attitude while you serve the public goes a long way to further the Kingdom. If you work with money or machines, doing your tasks well might make a difference in the lives of people you do not even know. The truth is that we can work out our vocation as disciples in any setting if we are focused on allowing God's Spirit to work in us and through us.

Even though I considered my job as a security guard to be mindless and meaningless, through it I found the time to discover my vocation. I spent the better part of two years wandering around that complex at night. It was a time in my life when I was struggling with my faith and with direction. After a while, I began to use all that quiet time to listen to God and eventually came to see those long nights as a gift. It was there in those dark hallways that I began to experience God's call on my life—a call to a new vocation of ministry. Soon I was back attending church after some years away, got into a Bible study, and eventually landed a job as a part-time youth director in another church. All that late night wandering eventually led me to ordained ministry and a whole new vocation.

Whatever you do for a living, if the Spirit of the Lord is upon you, you can do it for God's glory and to further God's purposes for the world. May you see your vocation as a gift from God!

What vocation is God calling you toward today?

PURPOSEFUL PATIENCE
1 THESSALONIANS 5:16-24

One of the churches I served as a youth minister had a tradition of taking an out-of-state mission trip every summer. It was a great way to provide the youth with an experience of service while helping them bond together as a group during the journey.

One year we decided to travel from Colorado Springs to San Francisco to serve in a mission with homeless people. After doing some research, I proposed to the group that traveling to California by train would be a fun, unique, and scenic journey across the West. They were enthusiastic about it, but they were enthusiastic about anything that got them out of the house for a week in the summer.

According to the rail line's timetable, the trip would take about 24 hours—about the same amount of time that it would take to drive. By train the journey could be made without all the hassle and hazard of keeping drivers awake and gas tanks filled. When the day came, we went to the train station in Denver and waited for the 8:00 P.M. train. After getting the baggage checked in, we heard over the loudspeaker that the *California Zephyr* was delayed and probably would not be there until midnight. The train showed up at 2:00 A.M.

Once we boarded and started moving, we soon learned that the timetable posted in the cars was more of a rough guideline than a schedule. The train stopped often in the middle of nowhere to let a freight express through, and we had to change engines a couple of times due to mechanical problems. The snack car ran out of food in the middle of Nevada. We were seated in coach, so about half way through the trip (or so we thought) the 30 of us looked like zombies and smelled foul after hours of not sleeping and not taking showers. The train finally pulled into Sacramento, where we were renting vans for the rest of the trip, ten hours late. That line

from a Tom Petty song kept running through my mind: "The waiting is the hardest part."[1]

We drove into San Francisco the next day, still beat from the trip. After bedding down in the church where we were staying, I got that gentle tap on the door from one of the female leaders saying that one of the girls was having stomach cramps and needed to go to the emergency room. It was midnight, and I drove through inner city San Francisco looking for a hospital. When we found one, we signed in and sat in the waiting room next to a guy with a metal fragment lodged in his head. We waited there until 4:00 A.M., which was a stark reminder to me of why people who wait in waiting rooms are called patients.

Our sick youth was finally seen and given a prescription that had to be filled immediately. We wound our way through the streets again looking for an all-night pharmacy, which was, mercifully, not too far from the church. All the while I was thinking about how tired I was, and I was kicking myself by realizing that we would have to do that eternal and infernal train trip in reverse going back home. I crawled into my sleeping bag on the floor at 5:00 A.M., only to be awakened at 6:30 to start the day's service. My youth group member? She woke up feeling great. I drained an entire pot of coffee.

I don't know about you, but I am not exactly a patient perso

Waiting, being in a situation beyond my control, is frustrating. Maybe some of us feel that way because we live in a world of microwave ovens, instant messaging, and overnight delivery. Waiting just does not seem necessary any more, so when our plans are altered and circumstances force us into a holding pattern, we feel anxious. We do not know what to do with ourselves, so we fret and get angry and maybe even lash out at the people around us.

What we often fail to realize is that waiting can be an opportunity. While we cannot always control our circumstances, we can always control our attitudes. The apostle Paul spent a lot of time waiting in prison cells and on storm-tossed ships. For him, however, waiting was not about getting anxious; it was about getting busy. The Thessalonians, like other Christians, were waiting for "the coming of our Lord Jesus Christ," for the kingdom of God to become a reality (1 Thessalonians 5:23). In these closing verses from his first letter to them, Paul gives instructions on what we might call "active waiting."

"Rejoice always," says Paul. Pray at all times, and be thankful no matter what circumstance in which you might find yourselves (verses 16-18). Paul had learned to sing hymns in dark prison dungeons (Acts 16:25) and had seen the circumstances of a shipwreck as an opportunity to minister to people on the island of Malta (Acts 28:1-10).

Paul had refused to give into anxiety and despair, seeing these interruptions in his mission as God-sent opportunities. There was no passivity in Paul, no sitting around hoping for something favorable to happen. When in doubt, Paul got busy doing "the will of God in Christ Jesus" (1 Thessalonians 5:18).

Paul warned the Thessalonians about the alternative view of waiting, too. Anxiety and anger can "quench the Spirit" and open avenues for evil to creep into our thoughts. A member of my congregation works as a gate agent for a major airline, and he told me that people who are forced to miss a flight due to an unforeseen circumstance begin to act with irrational hostility. "I try to tell them that yelling at me won't help," he says, "but they aren't thinking straight. Try as I might, I just can't stop a snowstorm in Chicago." He is often the victim of verbal abuse and threats, but he always has a ready response. "I just smile," he says. "They don't know what to do with that."

Instead of becoming anxious, we are to get busy keeping our "spirit . . . soul and body . . . sound and blameless" (verse 23) in preparation for the coming of Christ. Instead of approaching an imperfect world with anger or turning to sinful behavior as an escape or an excuse, we are to focus on being faithful to the one who has called us (verse 24). Think of waiting as a chance to offer the world a smile and turn every circumstance into an opportunity for God's grace, God's kingdom, to come shining through.

The train trip home was another marathon, but the good news was that we were only six hours late into Denver. As we reflected back on the experience, all of us on that trip realized that those hours spent in a train car were powerfully significant. I got to know some of those youth on a deep level and had life-altering conversations about God that we could not have had at a Sunday night youth fellowship meeting. We laughed, created new games, and supported one another when spirits were low. I have had the privilege of officiating at several weddings of young adults who were on that trip. When I hear from some of them by e-mail, even years later, any mention of a train brings a smile. The stories from that time of waiting are precious.

Advent teaches us that waiting time is precious time to prepare our hearts, minds, and attitudes, not only to prepare for the coming of Christ but to face an anxious world with a message of grace and hope. If we use our time wisely, we can look at the waiting as the best part of the season.

What is making you anxious today? How can a change of attitude alter how you wait?

POINTING TO JESUS
JOHN 1:6-8, 19-28

My son recently joined a youth flag football league in our town. My wife and I figured that flag football was OK given that our son, like his father, has the kind of slight physical stature that requires careful consideration before stepping out into a strong wind. I took him to the first practice and was glad it was flag, not tackle, football, since some of the third through fifth graders standing around in cleats looked like they could drive.

The coach for the Chargers is a woman who loves the game and is way more knowledgeable about the nuts and bolts of the game than I am. I spent most of my school years playing in the band at halftime instead of on the sidelines.

The Monday before the first Friday game, the coach called and asked if I would fill in for her since she had been called out on a business trip on short notice. That meant I would have to organize the team in practice, draw up some basic plays (we had not gotten that far yet in the other practices), and manage 13 kids, some of whom had never picked up a football in their short lives. I said, "Sure, I think I can handle that." Maybe it was that dad gene that makes you think you know everything, or maybe it was some secret buried fantasy about being a football coach prowling the sidelines with a headset and a clipboard. I don't know what made me agree to it, but I realized I had to get busy.

Wednesday afternoon I scrawled out six plays; and they were named, very originally, Plays 1-6. The odd plays would go left; the even ones would go right. For defense, well, I figured I would just get the kids to cover somebody. If these other kids are like mine, their short-term memory is not developed quite yet. I am pleased if they remember to wear shoes.

At practice, however, I realized that while I had done a decent job of putting in a game plan, I had not prepared for the enthusiastic egoism of a group of pre-adolescents. I blew the whistle and gathered the team around to give my inspirational opening speech; but instead I found myself in the midst of a bouncing mass of children with hands upraised and mouths open like a nest full of baby birds all asking, desperately, if they could please, please, *please* be the quarterback. Half of them did not know what a quarterback actually does, but they knew enough about football to deduce that that particular position was the center of attention. After all, offensive linemen are not generally the ones who get picked to do TV commercials.

I had to make a sudden shift from coach to psychologist, trying to convince a few tiny and tearful eight-year-olds that playing defensive back was as important as calling the signals. Add to that some parents stepping on to the practice field to give me some "advice" on where to play their child, and I remembered why I liked being in the marching band so much better.

We live in a culture of celebrity, so it should not be surprising that our children aspire to be the star. Adults are no different, really, often doing whatever is necessary to climb to the top of their profession regardless of the cost to their families and sometimes even at the risk of their own integrity. We have been culturally conditioned not to accept a secondary role in anything. The truth is, though, that championship teams are not built by putting together a roster full of quarterbacks, nor is any company going to achieve its goals if everyone is acting as CEO. The key is fitting the right people with the right talents and abilities in the right positions. Effective roleplayers are essential to winning teams.

Probably no better historical example of a roleplayer exists than John the Baptizer. John was the forerunner of the Messiah, a witness to the light that was coming into a dark world. As the writer says in this wonderful theological prologue to John's Gospel, John the Baptizer "was not the light" himself, but one who would testify to it (John 1:7-8).

Tellingly, the word *witness* in Greek has the same root as the word *martyr* in English. John's witness and testimony would involve giving his whole life over to the mission of preparing the way for Jesus and his ministry. The testimony that John gave to the religious leaders who came out into the wilderness to grill him was a clear statement about his role in the messianic program that was unfolding. John, you will recall, was drawing crowds out into the wilds with his baptism and his preaching, calling people to repent in preparation for the one who was coming to bring God's justice and God's judgment to Israel.

While he may have dressed oddly and lived a hermit's lifestyle, John seemed to be popular with the people. It would have been understandable if he had become caught up in the hype and parlayed that popularity into his own messianic program. That is certainly what we would expect to see happen in our culture of celebrity. John's response, though, was simple and succinct: "I am not the Messiah," he said plainly (verse 20).

The religious leaders wondered why John had not taken on the messianic claim for himself. Like a bunch of anxious children, they gathered around him with hands raised asking questions. "Who are you?" they asked. Are you Elijah or one of the prophets? "What do you say about yourself?" (verses 21-22). The religious leaders could not quite fathom why John was baptizing people, since on some level that would appear to be the role of the Messiah or an Elijah figure or, at the very least, a prophet (verse 24).

Surely, he had to have some ambition beyond living in the desert and standing in the muddy water.

John, however, knew that he was no quarterback. He realized that God had not recruited him to be the one to carry the ball, the message of God's kingdom, forward to the whole world. John's personal mission statement was that of a secondary role player, "the one crying out in the wilderness" (verse 23) and setting the conditions for the coming of the true star—the light that was coming into the world.

Since football was not a metaphor in heavy use in the first century, John would later use the image of the best man at a wedding to describe his role. He was to be the "friend of the bridegroom" who "rejoices greatly at the bridegroom's voice" (3:29). The best man is there to lead the celebration, not be the center of attention. John's ministry was focused fully on humbly pointing beyond himself to Jesus (1:26-27). When Jesus arrived on the scene, John knew that his role was complete. "He must increase," said the faithful role player, "but I must decrease" (3:30).

When I first started in ministry, I asked an older and wiser clergy mentor if he had any advice for me as a newly ordained preacher. I will never forget what he said: "Bob, just remember that there's only one Messiah—and you ain't him." I confess that sometimes I have strayed from that advice.

I have wanted to put myself in the spotlight or solve problems by exerting more effort instead of spending time in prayer. The results look kind of like I would envision if I were to be put in at quarterback in an NFL game with 300-pound linemen bearing down on my terrified 150-pound self. It is not a pretty picture. I am much better playing the role to which all of us have been called—pointing to Jesus.

We lost the game that Friday, but the kids gave a good accounting of themselves. Curtis, our quarterback, ran for a touchdown; and the other kids swarmed him in the end zone. "Did you see the block I made so Curtis could run it in?"

said one of my little gap-toothed gridiron greats. I sure did. And you know, I think God smiles at us, too, when we realize that our lives are meant to pave the way for Jesus to come into our homes, our workplaces, our schools, and anywhere else we have the opportunity to serve. Let us celebrate Advent as a time of remembering our role in furthering the victory of Jesus and his kingdom!

What is the role to which God has called you?

---

[1]From "The Waiting" on the album *Hard Promises,* by Tom Petty and the Heartbreakers (Backstreet, 1981).

Building God's House

Scriptures for Advent: The Fourth Sunday

2 Samuel 7:1-11, 16
Romans 16:25-27
Luke 1:26-38

When I was in junior high, I signed up for wood shop, mostly because all the other guys did, too. Looking back, home economics would have been far more useful to me; but at the time I wanted to engage in the manly pursuit of building stuff. After seeing the mangled disasters I turned in, my shop teacher told me I had a better future in demolitions.

Building happens in many ways, though. In a life of faith, things always go better when God makes the plans and guides the work. The Scriptures for the fourth Sunday in Advent are not so much about bricks and mortar as they are about building a people and a future through the coming Messiah. David wanted to build God a temple, but God was more interested in building David's family as a vehicle through which the savior of Israel would come. An angel came with a message inviting Mary to house the Promised One in her own person, to be the God-bearer for the whole world. The story of Christmas would be built on her faithfulness. Paul wrote to the Romans to remind them that those who believe in the Christ are the ones who house the secret of a divine mystery in their hearts. The early church was built on that good news.

This week reminds us that God is not so much concerned about what we build with our hands but how we dwell with God in our hearts. After all, God is good at transforming raw materials into spectacular creations!

AVOIDING "CATHEDRAL FATIGUE"
2 SAMUEL 7:1-11, 16

A couple of summers ago I took a pilgrimage to England with some clergy colleagues to visit some of the important Methodist historic sites. We traveled all over the country in the footsteps of the Wesleys. Along the way we stopped at several historic churches and some of the massive English cathedrals that have dominated the landscape since medieval times. The cathedrals really captured my attention.

Now, cathedral touring does give a person some jaw-dropping moments—tall spires, soaring ceilings, and high altars that were lovingly and painstakingly built to honor the awesomeness of God. When you think about how old some of these places are, it puts that whole "great cloud of witnesses" thing into perspective. Keep in mind, however, that old means something completely different in Europe than it does in the United States. In Europe, they measure history by centuries. In Lincoln, for example, our guides kept pointing out the new building addition on the east end of the cathedral that had replaced a part destroyed when the central tower catastrophically collapsed all the way through the floor of the building (I made a mental note to have our trustees check the church steeple as soon as I got home). This "new" addition, they announced proudly, was *just* completed in the year 1280.

It was a privilege to visit these historic centers of worship, but after a steady diet of about a cathedral a day for more than two weeks, I have to confess that they all started to run together. Too much of a good thing, even if it involves church, is still too much. It was somewhere in the nave at Bristol Cathedral that I realized that my own buttresses were no longer flying and I just wanted to crash. Relating this to one of my colleagues, she deftly diagnosed my malaise as "cathedral fatigue."[1]

I thought about that term a lot when I got back home and went back to work. Ministry involves a lot of building—building a community of faith, building programs to serve people, and even building and maintaining physical buildings. We typically plunge ahead into that work, doing everything that seems good because we are ostensibly doing it for God. We think that a high level of activity and productivity is what God expects from us, so we work harder and go faster from Sunday to Sunday, program to program, and mission to mission. The result is often a deep and pervasive sense of cathedral fatigue. We want to do a lot of things for God, but here is the question: Have we bothered to ask God what God wants us to do?

That is the question at the heart of this story of King David's desire to build a temple for God. As 2 Samuel 7 opens, David has been busy building his kingdom. He had conquered Jerusalem and established the capital of the monarchy there (2 Samuel 5:6-10). He brought the ark of the covenant, the very symbol of God's presence and God's covenant with Israel, into the new capital city (6:1-19). He had defeated all of his enemies and built his own "house" in the form of a palace made of expensive cedar wood (7:1-2).

Having completed all of that work, David still had one more task he wanted to fulfill—to move the ark out of its temporary home in a tent and build a grand temple to house it, and, by association, to provide a permanent dwelling place for God. After all, David was now living in a comfortable house; and, in his mind, God should have one, too (verse 2). This seemed to David a good plan, a reasonable plan, a plan that would certainly honor God. The prophet Nathan agreed. "Go, do all that you have in mind; for the Lord is with you" (verse 3).

One of my favorite movies is *Field of Dreams,* where Kevin Costner's character is told by a voice to build a baseball diamond in the middle of his Iowa cornfield. "If you build it, he will come," says the voice. No heavenly voice was calling David to build a temple for God, but David may have figured that if he built a temple then God would come in and live there.

God's response? Not so fast. God came to Nathan at night and gave the prophet a message for the king. "Are you the one to build me a house to live in?" asks God, perhaps a little sarcastically (verse 5). For generations, God had been "moving about in a tent and a tabernacle" wherever the Israelites wandered. God had never asked any of David's ancestors to build a temple, so why would David think God needed one now? God had

called David, been with him through all the conflict with Saul and through battles with Israel's enemies (verses 8-9). Why should David now be impatient and jump-start a process that God had not even whispered about to him?

David's intentions were certainly good, but God's intentions for David were better. A temple could wait. God had other building projects in mind, namely, building a "house" for David—a family line that would bring honor to David and peace to Israel (verses 9-11). Through David's house, his kingdom would be established forever (verse 13). Despite any "iniquity" David's royal descendants would commit (and the biblical record of the monarchy is that they were pretty good at committing iniquity), God's steadfast love would not be taken away from David's house (verses 14-15). David was not to spend his energy on building a cathedral; his son would do that (verses 12-13). Instead he was to focus on fulfilling the covenant promise of God.

Solomon would build the Temple, but the real fulfillment of God's promise to David would not involve bricks and mortar. Temples and cathedrals, after all, are not so permanent. Solomon's spectacular temple would be destroyed by the Babylonians in 586 B.C., be rebuilt again after the Exile, and destroyed again by Herod the Great before Jesus was born. The Romans would destroy it permanently in A.D. 70. The real

Temple, the real dwelling place for God, was never meant to be a monument or a museum like many European cathedrals have become. God's dwelling with humanity would instead be in a person, in Jesus Christ; and through him God would come to live not just *with* God's people but live *in* them, too.

Someone once said that if you want to make God laugh, tell God your plans. God must get a kick out of all the grandiose plans we make for our lives and for our churches. We are so busy making plans for God that we often fail to listen for the plans that God is making for us. In many ways, prayer is more important than productivity. That is the cure for cathedral fatigue.

At Lincoln Cathedral, I was walking near the shrine to St. Hugh, who was instrumental in building and expanding the cathedral in the late 12th century. As I walked past the shrine, I tripped over two deep grooves in the floor. I asked the guide what was up with this architectural anomaly, and her answer was very telling. "That groove," she said, "was made by the feet of thousands of pilgrims who have knelt at this very spot to pray for more than 700 years." Temples come and go, people come and go; but God's word, God's plan, God's dwelling with us, lasts forever. Better that we make prayer grooves in the floor than building monuments to our accomplishments.

If you are feeling cathedral fatigue during this Advent season, the best cure is to get on your knees. That is where we hear the real message of what God wants us to be and to do.

What are ways you can beat cathedral fatigue in your life? in your church? What "house" is God building in your life?

HEARING THE DIVINE WHISPER
ROMANS 16:25-27

One of the things I have come to realize as I have gotten older is that my brain's hard drive needs serious defragmentation, which you computer-savvy types would understand. For example, I can listen to the radio and remember the words to nearly every classic rock song from the '70's and '80's; but I cannot remember where I put my car keys this morning. I can remember commercial jingles from my childhood, but I cannot remember why I walked upstairs a few minutes ago. I am sitting here in my study still trying to figure it out.

One of the commercials from the early '80's that is burned on my brain used to run during the soap opera my college roommates and I watched every afternoon. I shudder to think that we spent our precious study time caring about the narcissistic travails of unusually attractive people, but we were young and in serious need of a life. Anyway, a commercial for Whisper perfume came on during every show. The ad may have been geared toward women, but it hit the early 20's male demographic square in the eyeballs. A stunningly beautiful young woman would appear on the screen in an extreme close-up; and she would say slowly in a low, husky, come-hither voice, "If you want to get someone's attention . . . *whissperr.*" Well, she had my attention.

In this case there was definite truth in advertising. This commercial took advantage of a basic truth about communication. If you want to get someone's attention, whispering is one of the most effective techniques you can employ. Public speakers know that the best way to get people to lean into what they are saying is to vary the pitch of your voice and occasionally drop it to a whisper. If people in the audience lean over to the person next to them and cup their hand around the recipient's ear to whisper, speakers can become distracted and wonder what they are whispering about, especially if they look at the speaker and laugh.

When I was a youth minister, hearing whispers in a church camp cabin at 2:00 A.M. certainly piqued my interest in that particular conversation. Whispering usually means that something interesting is going on, and we want to know what it is. I did not buy the perfume because I did not have any-body to give it to at the time, but I never forgot the message.

That commercial keeps coming back to me during these days of Advent because I think that God is much more of a whisperer than a shouter. The apostle Paul expressed the thought in the final doxology in his letter to the Romans (16:25). For Paul, God's plan of salvation for the world was a long-kept secret, whispered into the ears of prophets and played out in the desert wanderings of God's people throughout the centuries. The mystery of God's revelation in Jesus Christ was now being disclosed to the Gentiles, getting the attention of people everywhere (Romans 16:25-26). The proclamation of the good news, that Jesus Christ is Lord, would enable people of every nation to see the veil of mystery between God and humanity pulled back; and what was revealed was surprising. The secret was that God had come to humanity in the person of a humble peasant contractor from the backwater town of Nazareth on the edge of the Roman Empire. No one had expected that!

Contrary to popular belief, our God is generally not a thundering, booming, noisy God who commands our attention with lightning bolts and loud apocalyptic pronouncements. Sure the Bible reveals that God certainly has the ability to communicate in this way, but God usually uses quieter means. People in Paul's day (and in ours, for that matter) would have expected God's entry into the world to come by way of a cosmic fanfare and cloud assault, complete with pyrotechnics and a awesome action-movie soundtrack—a la Arnold Schwarzenegger. Imagine the ascension of Jesus in that context: "Ah'll be baack."

God, however, is way more subtle. A story is told of a young man who asked a rabbi, "Why did God speak to Moses from a thorn bush?" For the man thought that God should have spoken instead in a peal of thunder on the peak of some majestic mountain. The rabbi answered, "To teach you that there is no place on earth where God's glory is not, not even in a humble thorn bush."

Do we believe that there is no time, no place, and no event so earthly that God cannot be there, whispering through them? The divine presence that resides in every aspect of earthly life will go unnoticed unless we realize the meek, unassuming, and secretive way that God characteristically comes. It is the divine whisper that speaks.

Children can teach us a lot about subtle communication, particularly when it comes to listening to God. When our daughter, Hannah, was a toddler, we made the mistake of putting our wooden Nativity set under the Christmas tree where she could easily reach it. One day as I was looking under the tree for presents to shake, I noticed that Mary and Joseph, the shepherds, and the wise men were all looking lovingly down at an empty manger. Baby Jesus was missing.

I started looking all over the house for the Messiah—in cabinets, under furniture, behind doors, in the VCR. (I found animal crackers in there once, so it was a valid place to look). The King of kings was nowhere to be found.

A little later that evening I was putting some of Hannah's toys away when I noticed her little yellow Fisher Price school bus in the corner. Looking inside, I noticed that the bus had the usual passengers—the bald Fisher Price doctor, the construction worker with his little hard hat, a policeman, a mommy pushing a baby carriage, and the bus driver. They were all smiling in their places; but there in the third seat back on the right was Baby Jesus with a big smile on his face, too. I was struck by the realization that my tiny child had solved the mystery of the Incarnation in her own special way. She seemed to know that Baby Jesus did not come to stay in a manger but belonged on the bus, hanging out with all those smiling people. Come to think of it, putting that Nativity set under the tree was not a mistake at all. It was simply another opportunity to hear the still, small voice of God through the wonder of a child.

It is the still, small voice of God that speaks real, life-transforming truth. Psalm 46:10 says, "Be *still*, and know that I am God!" It is in the silence; in the waiting; in the empty, back-alley recesses of our spirit; on a bus full of smiling wooden people that God is most able to speak the divine whisper to us. The Gospel of John begins by calling Jesus "the Word"—the word that defines and reveals the hidden God. We need to create space for that Word to enter our lives.

You want a great exercise for Advent? Take the Baby Jesus out of your Nativity set, and carry him to work or school with you today. People might be whispering about your apparent weirdness, but you will know the real secret. After all, that is where he belongs—God with us.

How will you take Jesus with you as you go about your work today? How can you create space to hear God's Word, God's whisper in your life?

LIVING
A GOD-BEARING LIFE
LUKE 1:26-38

We have been having quite a baby boom at our church over the last couple of years, with many new moms and dads toting their tiny ones into worship and filling the nursery. On one particular Sunday last fall, we had 21 babies in the nursery, which caused a major meltdown for the staff. I was told that if you happened to be walking down the hall of the education wing that Sunday, you were likely handed a baby to hold and bounce. Apparently, when one cries they all decide to join the choir.

Utah has one of the highest birth rates in the nation, which should not be surprising given that this is the state that brought the Osmond family to national prominence. I have learned, though, that we are a bit of an anomaly. Statistically speaking, people are having fewer children than they did just a few decades ago; and economically speaking the US Department of Agriculture says that the cost of raising a child from birth through the age of 17 can run up to between $196,000 to $393,000—and that does not include college.[2] Being a parent is not just an act of love; it is an investment. No wonder these smiling parents coming to church on Sunday morning seem to be a little extra focused during prayer time.

Most of the young families I meet have carefully prepared. They have done the math, worked the timetable, and juggled the job responsibilities to make room for that little bundle of joy. There are others, though, such as the single soon-to-be mom, who are trying to make it on their own and want desperately to give their children good homes. That mother's excitement is tempered by the realization of all the responsibility. No matter how much you prepare, having a child is a big deal.

We read the story of Gabriel's visit to Mary, and it is easy for us to forget that Mary was just a kid herself. Girls in first-century Israel were usually married by the age of 12 or 13, about the time girls these days are just beginning to notice that boys are not complete goof-balls. Mary was engaged and living in a culture where the shame of being pregnant out of wedlock could result in the woman being at best ostracized and at worst stoned to death. Being told that you were going to have a baby under unusual and potentially dangerous circumstances was one thing, but Gabriel told Mary also that this would not be just any baby— he would be *the* Baby. The Child she would bear would be the ful-fillment of God's covenant with David (Luke 1:36-33), the Messiah who would save the world. Talk about your major announcements!

We certainly could not blame Mary if she had simply said, "No, thanks." She could have turned into a first-century version of a runaway bride. Instead, she only asked one question: "How can this be, since I am a virgin?" (verse 34). The angel said that God's Spirit would "come upon" Mary and God's power would "overshadow" her, making the Child soon to be in her womb special indeed. This Child would be called "Son of God" (verse 35).

Do not miss the pure dynamite, the real baby "boom" in that latter acclamation. As if Mary's situation was not tenuous enough, the title

that her Child would bear made his future even more so.

In the first century, at the time Jesus was born, there was already one person in the world with the title "Son of God," and that was the Roman emperor Augustus. Augustus was the first Roman emperor to be considered divine, and the cult of the emperor was a simple fact of life in the Empire. Augustus's face was minted on coins, and his name appeared on road markers throughout the Mediterranean world. To suggest that there was another Son of God was to, in effect, commit treason against the empire. The Baby that Mary would bear would, through his teaching and ministry, chal-lenge the way of the Empire—the way of violence, the way of power, the way of prosperity for the few and poverty for the many. He would die on a Roman cross, a symbol of ultimate defeat at the hands of the Empire; but God would turn that into victory. Gabriel was announcing that the true Son of God was coming into the world.

I like to think that Mary care-fully considered the implications of what the angel was saying. If she had any doubts about what it all meant, she would have certainly understood it later at the Baby's dedication in the Temple, when Simeon told her that the Child would be "a sign to be opposed" and that a "sword would pierce [her] own soul, too" (2:34-35). Despite all the difficulty, the uncertain future, the possibility of bringing shame on herself and her family, the pain of childbirth, and the long-term commitment, Mary said yes to the task she was being given. "Here am I, the servant of the Lord," she said. "Let it be with me according to your word" (1:38).

I have been collecting icons for a few years now, and one that hangs prominently in my office depicts Mary holding the Child Jesus. The icon is titled with the Greek word that the Eastern Orthodox churches use to describe her: *Theotokos,* which means "God-bearer." That is a perfect description of what Mary did in giving her consent to the divine mission she was being offered. In saying yes to God, she became the God-bearer, allowing her person to be the means of bringing the life of God into the world.

Remember that when the angel greeted Mary, he addressed her as "favored one" (1:28). It was not that Mary was particularly righteous or worthy, though some Christian traditions have assumed that understanding. Notice earlier in the chapter that Elizabeth and Zechariah, parents of John the Baptizer, are characterized as being "righteous before God, living blamelessly according to all the commandments and regulations of the Lord" (verse 6). Mary did not receive such accolades from Luke, yet she is favored or blessed with the task of bearing the Messiah. It was not her character that made

her worthy, though I am fairly sure she was faithful based on her response. Instead, like her ancestor Abraham, God favored Mary—an ordinary girl in an ordinary place—and blessed her so she might be a blessing to the world, a vital link in the covenant chain that God had begun with Abraham generations before (Genesis 12:2). God's favor is not something we earn; it is something we receive as a gift, but a gift that must always be shared.

This story challenges those of us who have received the gift of a relationship with Jesus to be God-bearers to the rest of the world, believing that God's grace always comes to us on its way to someone else. We bear the Christ, we share God's grace, and we change the world when we take on Mary's attitude of service and surrender. We would do well to memorize and use her response as we move about in the world every day.

Think about it. You are in the grocery store, and a mom with several anxious children is behind you in the register line. She is at her wit's end, just needing to get to the car and get her crying toddler home for a nap. You are busy and in a hurry, too; but here is a perfect opportunity to step out of line and say, "Here am I, the servant of the Lord."

You are at work, and the boss is hassling you again. You want to quit, you want to tell him off, you want to explode. What difference would it make in your attitude, or even in your boss, for you to say, "Here am I, the servant of the Lord"?

You have a thousand tasks to do today and no time to do them. You want to crawl back in bed and pull the covers over your head. Imagine what would happen, though, if you started every day by saying, "Here am I, the servant of the Lord." Chances are you would see problems as opportunities for God's grace to shine through.

I encourage you to memorize Mary's God-bearing response and use it every day during this Advent season. Make it a habit and watch how the love of God goes "boom" in your world!

Where do you need to say, "Here am I, a servant of the Lord"? How can you be a God-bearer to your family, your co-workers, and others?

[1] From "Cathedral Fatigue," by Bob Kaylor, in *Homiletics*, January-February, 2007; page 8.
[2] From "Expenditures on Children, 2007," by The United States Department of Agriculture (US Department of Agriculture Center for Nutrition Policy and Promotion, 2007); pages 12-13 (*http://www.cnpp.usda.gov/Publications/CRC/crc2007.pdf*).

Come and Behold Him

Scriptures for Christmas Eve:
Isaiah 9:2-7
Titus 2:11-14
Luke 2:1-20

The church that I served in seminary used to do a live Nativity scene each year the week before Christmas. Since I was the youth pastor, it was my job to organize the youth to portray Mary, Joseph, the shepherds, and the wise men. Baby Jesus was always portrayed by a plastic doll we found in the church nursery. We did our live Nativity outside the church in a makeshift stable that was drenched in copious amounts of the sleet and rain that usually marked the Christmas season in western Ohio. We had a pen with live sheep and goats, which provided a multi-sensory effect to the whole scene.

The church sat on a little two-lane road; and it always amazed me that on the nights we presented the Nativity, cars would come streaming in to see it in spite of bad weather. "We just got done shopping," said one man as he pulled a rain hood over his head. "We stopped here so that we could remember what the whole thing is about."

The Scriptures for Christmas Eve call us to do the same thing. The story is familiar but is always fresh in the retelling. Wherever we are going with our lives, the Christmas story is a call to pull over, stop, and remember what the whole thing is about: celebrating a Savior who is born for us all.

COME TO THE LIGHT
ISAIAH 9:2-7

One of my favorite summer activities when I was a boy was spending a week with my grandparents, who lived on a little farm in rural western Pennsylvania. The village near where they lived was populated with several of my other relatives, including a whole pack of cousins who were my age. We spent those summer days playing baseball from sunup to sundown in a field full of undulating mounds of earth and groundhog holes, occasionally losing a ball in the high weeds that bordered the woods in right field.

We would play until it was dark enough that one of us would get hit on the noggin with an unseen ball and the one street light in the village would flicker on. It was usually at that point I realized it was pitch dark and the only way back to the farm was a single-lane road through a mile of forest.

This was the early 1970's; and one of the TV shows that came on every week was called *In Search Of*, with Leonard Nimoy as the host. The show explored unexplained phenomena such as the Loch Ness Monster, UFOs, and—most frightening for me—Bigfoot. I had seen the show, and Nimoy's spooky narration and grainy video images had me absolutely convinced that Bigfoot had migrated from the Pacific Northwest and was waiting to grab me as I rode my single-speed bike up the road to the safety of the farm. I put a light on the handlebars to try and make myself feel better, but it only made the world outside the little cone of light even darker.

I could almost feel Bigfoot breathing down on my neck as I cleared the tree line and headed toward the lights of the farmhouse, fighting my fear of the dark as Leonard Nimoy's voice ran through my head. The next day, though, I would do it all over again. The light of day always put things into perspective and made those woods look a lot less like a Bigfoot habitat.

Humans have long feared the night, particularly in the days before electricity could artificially extend daylight. Stories of monsters and deadly foes waiting unseen in the darkness have been part of our lore for centuries, and the contrast between darkness and light is an often-used metaphor for the contrast between good and evil. The Bible itself is full of references to darkness and light from the first chapter of Genesis onward. The prophet Isaiah calls upon these images to describe the movement of the people of Judah from a time of fear into a time of hope and prosperity, an event predicated on the birth of a new king.

As Isaiah 9 opens, the nation of Judah is under a dark cloud of fear because the armies of the Assyrian empire under King Tiglath-pileser had been running them down like some ancient imperial Bigfoot. The Assyrians had already conquered the tribal regions of Zebulun and Naphtali, the coastal regions around Mount Carmel, and the region east of the Galilee. Judah and Jerusalem would be next (verse 1). The prophecy of First Isaiah, however, was that a new king had been born who would recapture those lands, unite the kingdoms of Israel and Judah, and usher in an era of peace. Verses 2-7 appear to be a hymn of coronation for this new king, which may have been Hezekiah, though he is not specifically named. The words of the hymn were applied to the reign of future kings in the Davidic line and, by the time of the first century, to the anticipated Messiah. The birth of a new ruler was a cause for hope, a light dawning in the midst of darkness.

The vision that the prophet offers is nothing less than the end of oppression and war. The "rod of their oppressor" would be broken and the implements of warfare would be burned "as fuel for the fire" (verses 4-5). These are prophecies that would certainly bring joy to a people under the threat of military domination, but they came to mean even more than that. Isaiah's vision seems to be more universal, looking forward to a day when the darkness of war and destruction would be forever washed away by the light of God's peace.

The new ruler had divine authority to bring this vision to reality (verse 6). The understanding at the time of Isaiah was that the kings of Judah became reborn as God's son at the time of their coronation, a tradition that had begun with Solomon (2 Samuel 7:14; Psalm 2:7-9; 89:19-29). The titles that the king would assume reflected this divine-human relationship: "Wonderful Counselor, Mighty God, / Everlasting Father, Prince of Peace" (Isaiah 9:6). These were titles that were similar to those given to Egyptian pharaohs at their coronation, which may indicate that Judah's kings were regarded as divine as

were the rulers of other nations in the ancient Near East. The key here, though, is that the Davidic king's success would be predicated on the zeal of God to establish justice and righteousness through his rule (verse 7).

The kings of Judah were not able to live up to the promise of Isaiah's prophecy. Hezekiah would bring religious reforms and repair Solomon's Temple after years of neglect under his apostate ancestors. He would hold off the Assyrians and preserve Jerusalem from capture with the help of divine action (2 Kings 18–19). Even so, Hezekiah would eventually succumb to illness and his son Manasseh would undo most of his reforms (2 Kings 20). Isaiah's hymn of coronation may have been trotted out with each new king, but more often than not the words would ring hollow as the kings repeatedly failed. Darkness, and the fear it brought, always seemed to follow a period of daylight. Then, as now, humans do not seem to learn the lesson and wait until the darkness closes in before making a desperate run back to God.

God, however, is not afraid of the dark. God's reign of justice is like a sunrise that ever so gradually brings light to all the dark corners of the world. While the human rulers failed, God did not. In fact, God chose to make this ancient hymn a reality by fulfilling it forever in the person of his own true Son. Like his royal ancestors, Jesus came as a helpless and vulnerable child; but unlike the other kings, he would illuminate all people with the light of God's eternal kingdom. In his birth, a new day was dawning.

The world remains a dark and scary place. Bigfoot may or may not be just a legend (the jury is still out on that, in my opinion), but scarier monsters surround us: war, poverty, genocide, oppression, and injustice, just to name a few. Only the true King can shed light on them and bring the perspective of God's plan to redeem the world. He does not call us to run for our lives from these monsters but to face them and counter them with a vision of God's peace.

"The light shines in the darkness," John said about Jesus, "and the darkness did not overcome it" (John 1:5). May we come to the manger this Advent and be illuminated by the one true King.

What are some of your fears about the future? How does the birth of Jesus shed light on those fears?

COME SHARE THE GIFT
TITUS 2:11-14

For preachers, Christmas Eve is like Super Bowl Sunday—the big game that we start preparing for even earlier than the stores start putting up their holiday displays. We order all our Christmas bulletin covers in October, and every year we get just a few more in anticipation of the crowds that will come to church. Dancing in many a preacher's head are visions of Billy Graham-like conversion numbers and the transformation of H2O attendees (that's "Holidays, 2 Only") into highly committed followers of Jesus; and, if a true miracle occurs, junior-high Sunday school teachers. Well, at least one can pray.

Reality, however, is a bit stickier. Most clergy will have to preach that sermon two or three times (or more). I know that by the midnight service (my fourth of the night) I have sucked on so many cough drops that I have this intense urge to yodel. The cacophonous din of rustling bulletins, insistent latecomers, and screaming babies drown out that whole "no crying he makes" line in "Away in a Manger." We will have crammed 450 people into a space meant for 250, give each of them a lit candle, and pray that no one gets so excited that they accidentally burn someone. At the end of it all, I usually stumble home around 1:00 A.M., munch on the stale cookies and warm milk the kids left for Santa, and realize that I still have to put out the presents and tackle that "some assembly required" gift project. So much for a "Silent Night."

If we are honest with ourselves in October, we look toward Christmas knowing that while a few of those many visitors will find their way back to church, most of them will not be in the pew again until Easter. People tend to like babies and bunnies and a kind of ho-ho-holiness more than the daily grind of committed discipleship; and, sure as Christmas comes once a year, your church custodian will be spending the week before New Year's in the annual ritual of trying to get the spilled candle wax off the sanctuary carpet. It is tempting to wonder why we go to all the trouble.

Perhaps that is why the lectionary places this little passage from Paul's letter to Titus in the mix of texts for Christmas Eve. It is not the grand and familiar story of Mary and Joseph journeying to Bethlehem or Isaiah's magnificent vision of a world where justice and peace replace war and oppression as the primary news stories. Those are certainly more dramatic readings. Titus, on the other hand, is beautiful for its simplicity in summing up the whole reason for celebrating Christmas in a single line: "For the grace of God has appeared, bringing salvation to all" (Titus 2:11).

Theologically speaking, *grace* is a shorthand way of talking about God's unmerited favor, God's love, patience, forgiveness, and peace offered to us as a gift that appeared in a manger in Bethlehem. That gift was a voluntary offering of God who, in Christ, "gave himself for us" (verse 14). Grace is not only a theological concept but a God-embodied example that enables us to be redeemed from the guilt of our sin and embrace the hope of salvation that God has promised us.

Notice, however, that God's gift of grace was never meant simply to qualify us for an individual heavenly reward, a point upon which many Christian theologies want to focus. Paul uses the first-person plural to talk about the effects of God's grace for us *all.* Grace deals with our past—the "impiety" and "worldly passions" of life before following Christ. Having dealt with the past through God's forgiveness, grace also acts in the present to "live lives that are self-controlled, upright, and godly," in preparation for the future "blessed hope" of "the manifestation of the glory of our great God and Savior, Jesus Christ" (verses 12-13). In other words, God's grace is not just a nice gift to be opened and then shelved until we need it; instead it is designed to be *used,* to transform us so we can in turn transform the world. God's grace comes to us as a gift, but it is a gift we pass on to someone else.

I get excited talking about the gift of grace on Christmas Eve. The hyper-consumerism of our culture makes it hard for people to hear it because they are so used to being told every day that life is all about getting what they want. Christmas, on the other hand, teaches us that God has already given us everything we need: grace, love, forgiveness, a new start, and a new way of life. Talk about your useful gifts! We go to all that trouble on Christmas Eve because we know that in the end God's gift of grace in Jesus Christ is the only gift that matters.

I challenge you this Christmas Eve to look for those people who will come expecting just a little bit of ho-ho-holiness and offer them grace. Welcome them, learn their names, sit with them, and show them what life in Christ looks like when it is born in a person just like them. Offer them Christ in your words, your hospitality, and in your attitude. You have been given a gift, and there is no better time to share it.

How can you share the gift of God's grace with someone this Christmas Eve? How does your church offer Christ to those who will visit?

COME TO BETHLEHEM
LUKE 2:1-20

The road from Jerusalem to Bethlehem winds its way through residential areas and bustling business districts for about six miles or so. The closer you get to the place where Jesus was born, though, the scenery gives way to the sight of a long, high, concrete wall blocking the road. Bethlehem, you see, is in the West Bank—Palestinian territory. The Israeli government erected this wall in 2002 as a way of keeping suicide bombers from infiltrating into Israel. As you wait to enter the busy checkpoint, you notice the guards on the ground and in the towers, scanning the area with automatic weapons. You look out the window at the stark grey of the concrete wall, the razor wire, and tire-ripping barriers. However, what you really notice in the midst of all this military display of security is the brightly painted sign that spans the wall from nearly top to bottom by one of the guard towers. It is a sign that was put there by the Israeli Ministry of Tourism; and it says in English, Hebrew, and Arabic, "Peace Be With You," an interesting sentiment to be painted on a wall covered by a machine gun in a tower.

On the other side of the wall, the Palestinian side, the wall is not neatly painted with slogans for the tourists but is sprayed with graffiti in Arabic and English. "God will tear down this wall," says one. A giant spray-painted snake slithers down the length of the wall toward the checkpoint. There is a drawing of a young girl in pigtails and a pink dress patting down an Israeli soldier. On another section of the wall is a picture of a dove of peace wearing a flak jacket. Turning away from the wall you notice the stark contrast that comes by moving about 50 yards from Israeli territory into Bethlehem. It is almost like flipping a switch from prosperity to poverty.

To live in Bethlehem, on the other side of the wall, is to deal with staggeringly high unemployment. Those few who are fortunate enough to have jobs outside the city have to stand for hours in long lines every morning and evening to be searched and herded through the checkpoint on their way to and from work. Shops are boarded up, infrastructure is crumbling, and life depends on the trickle of tourists who are allowed through the wall to quickly visit the Church of the Nativity and maybe stop at one of the few gift shops selling olive wood Nativity sets. One wood carver, Tawfiq Salsaa, makes Nativity sets that look like the others except there is a wall separating the wise men and Jesus. "I wanted to give the world an idea of how we live in the Holy Land," says the 65-year-old Palestinian carpenter.[1] Truth is, if the wise men tried to get to Bethlehem today, they would have to run their gifts through a metal detector. On this side of the wall, life is hard.

When we read the Christmas story and when we sing "O Little Town of Bethlehem," this is not what we picture. We love the Christmas card image of a sleepy little town with open streets and gentle, rustic stables. While there was no concrete wall around Bethlehem in the first century, there was a stark contrast between the poor of this little village and the powerful holding court in Jerusalem and in Rome. Bethlehem and all of Israel was occupied territory.

The emperor, Augustus, ruled over most of the Mediterranean world. Augustus was the first Roman emperor to be considered divine. Some of his titles may sound familiar: son of God, savior of the world. The cult of the emperor was the main Roman religion, and his face was everywhere from coins to road markers. Augustus was called a man of peace, but his definition of peace was that of every empire that has ever moved across the face of the world. Peace was about victory and about military and economic security. Augustus killed off the opposition, took over foreign lands, and called it peace. He taxed those conquered peoples heavily in order to fund his army, his building projects, and his personal needs. Under Augustus, Rome erected a virtual wall of separation between those who were in and out, those who were rich and poor, and those who lived and died. Peace was the luxury of the powerful.

What we miss when we boil down the Christmas story to a once-a-year celebration of mangers and mall-shopping is the stark truth. Jesus was born on the wrong side of the wall. Note, however, that when the angels came they did not appear in Rome or in the Temple in Jerusalem. They did not perform a concert for the emperor or invade the dreams of wealthy merchants or military leaders. When the angels came, they came to Bethlehem and gave their performance for a group of shepherds who, in a place of poverty, were the poorest of the poor. It was to them, the lowest of the low, the insignificant and forgotten people of the Empire, that God chose to reveal his grand plan for the world.

The plan that God was announcing through the overture of the angel choir was a plan of peace but a peace radically different from that so often trumpeted by human empires. God's plan of peace on earth would not come through the power and might of conquering armies and vanquished enemies. It would not be a peace that meant prosperity for some and poverty for others. It was not peace through victory, but peace through God's justice. That is what *shalom*—the Hebrew word for "peace"—really means: well-being, justice, good news for *all* the people. It is the kind of peace that happens when God sits on the throne of the world and not Caesar. It is the kind of peace described in Isaiah 9:2-7 where the yoke of oppression is shattered and where the implements of war are "destined for burning." It is the kind of peace that Mary sings about in Luke 1:46-55, a song incorporated with that of the angels. She sang, "[God] has scattered the proud in the thoughts of their hearts. / He has brought down the powerful from their thrones, / and lifted up the lowly; / he has filled the hungry with good things, / and sent the rich away empty" (verses 51-53).

We sing of "peace on earth, good will toward men" along with the angels; but when the angels retreat back into heaven and we go home from the Christmas Eve service, we put away that vision for another year. World peace is a nice idea, but we wonder what we can actually *do* about it.

However, maybe we feel that way because we live on the other side of the wall from Bethlehem. Many of us live in places where we can spend our money on recreation instead of wondering where our next meal is coming from. We have the luxury of looking at places such as the Middle East, Darfur, and other locations around the world through our television screens instead of seeing war, genocide, injustice, and poverty just outside our windows. When it gets to be too much, we can afford to change the channel. The empire has been good for us, and because of that it is easy for us to forget about the world on the other side of the wall. The truth is, however, that that is precisely where Jesus is calling us.

Most people come to worship on Christmas Eve expecting to hear a message about a smiling baby, gentle shepherds, adoring parents, and lowing cattle. Perhaps they are looking for a little something to bless all the gift-buying they have done. After all, we are supposed to feel good at Christmas, right? The problem is, though, that the story of Christmas is about more than those things. Luke and the other Gospel writers wanted to take us through the gates of our own security and comfort to the other side of the wall. The Christmas carols call us to "come ye, O come ye to Bethlehem" and "come to Bethlehem and see." We sing that so easily; but in order to know what Christmas means, we have to go to Bethlehem—to cross our hearts and minds over to that side of the wall where we can hear the songs of angel choirs proclaiming that God is doing something about the real problems in the real world.

The Baby, born in a barn and laid in a manger, grew up preaching and embodying a message of the coming kingdom of God—God's reign and rule on the earth, a Kingdom that would bring justice and well-being to the whole world. He healed the sick, touched the untouchable, called people to share their wealth, and fed the hungry. He spent his time with outcasts, loved the unlovable, and washed the feet of his disciples like the lowliest servant. His mission and message drew fire from his enemies, whose version of comfort and security was threatened by his call for justice and grace. Rather than vanquish his enemies, though, he forgave them even as he was nailed to a Roman cross— the ultimate symbol of the Empire's ability to kill and destroy. After his death, the Empire walled him in a stone tomb and sealed the door shut. That is what empires do to those who challenge the status quo.

In Jesus, God showed that empires cannot and will not have the last word. That word belongs to the true King, the one for whom the angels sing; the true Son of God; the one called Wonderful, Counselor, Mighty God, Everlasting Father, and the true Prince of Peace. Jesus breaks down walls of violence and injustice; walls that separate rich and poor; walls that define who is worthy and who is not; and walls of sin and death that separate us from knowing the love, peace, and justice of God in this world.

To celebrate Christmas, then, is to celebrate hope that challenges empires and changes lives. It is about following Jesus in a mission that breaks down the walls of this world and makes God's kingdom a reality.

"Come to Bethlehem and see." How do we do it? It is not about traveling there, though I would highly recommend that you see it for yourself sometime. We cannot all campaign for office or be full-time activists. What we can do, however, is come to the manger to embrace Luke's story of Christmas, not as a once-a-year tradition but as a call upon our lives. We can offer our worship and ourselves to the Christ Child, trusting that his Kingdom of peace and justice will come through us. We can keep our eyes on the workings of empires and watch for the places where power fosters injustice. We can challenge empires with a message of *shalom.*

We can also listen for the song of the angels. That song is sung in the Bethlehems of the world; and we go there every time we serve the poor, fight injustice, speak for those who are voiceless, serve a meal to a hungry person, spend time in a prison teaching an inmate a new way of life, and in thousands of other little ways. Every great work begins with little steps.

Tawfiq Salsaa still makes his little olive wood Nativity sets with the wall between the wise men and baby Jesus; but even in occupied Bethlehem, even behind the wall, there is hope. Every wall in every Nativity set Tawfiq makes is removable. That is what Christmas is about: peace on earth—a peace with no more walls. Come to Beth-lehem and see. It is only there that you will learn what Christmas is all about.

What are the Bethlehems to which God may be calling you? How can you spread peace in your home, your school, your workplace?

---

[1] From "Three Wise Men Hit a Barrier in Bethlehem," by Rebecca Harrison at Reuters UK, December 12, 2007 (*http://uk. reuters.com/article/oddlyEnoughNews/idUKL1 026107520071212?feedType=RSS=oddly EnoughNews <http://uk.reuters.com/article/oddly EnoughNews/idUKL1026107520071212?feed Type=RSS&feedName=oddlyEnoughNews*).